VALUES FRIENDS

Mini Series

Age 6-9, Book 2

GLORIA PREMA

Copyright © 2002, 2016 and 2020
by Gloria Prema

All rights reserved.

www.ValuesFriends.net

First edition published in 2002 by OMbres Publishing, UK, and printed by AVC, Aberdeen, Scotland

Revised edition published in 2016 by OMbres Publishing, UK, and printed by CreateSpace, an Amazon.com company.

Mini series published in 2020 by kdp.amazon

Available from Amazon.com and other retail outlets
Available on Kindle and other devices

DEDICATION

For all children everywhere.

"There is no trust more sacred than the one the world holds with children."

Kofi Annan, 7th UN Secretary General (from 1997-2006), 2001 Nobel Peace Prize Winner

CONTENTS

TRUTH 1
LOVE 7
PEACE 13
RIGHT-CONDUCT ... 19
NON-VIOLENCE 25

TRUTH

I AM ME AND I AM FREE
EVERYONE IS SPECIAL IN THEIR OWN WAY
I AM PART OF THE UNIVERSE, AND THE
UNIVERSE IS PART OF ME
THINK, SPEAK AND ACT THE SAME
DOING MY BEST IS GOOD ENOUGH

TRUTH

If I can't do something then I try and try
My soul takes wings and I find I can fly
If I keep on going and never give up
Life rewards me with a golden cup.

The cup is filled with courage and dreams
And hope and strength and, although it seems
That it's never filled up to the top, as a rule
It's never half empty – it's always half full.

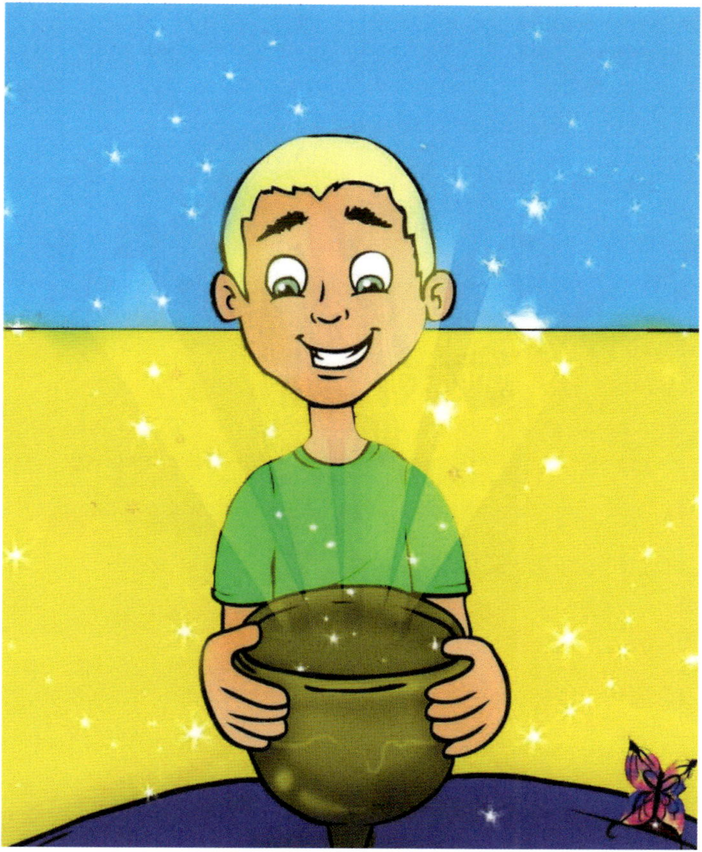

TRUTH

Feeling low, don't know which way to go
Look up, take a peek, maybe you'll see the answers you seek
Stand up, turn around, maybe this is where they're found
Jump up, do a dance, give yourself another chance.

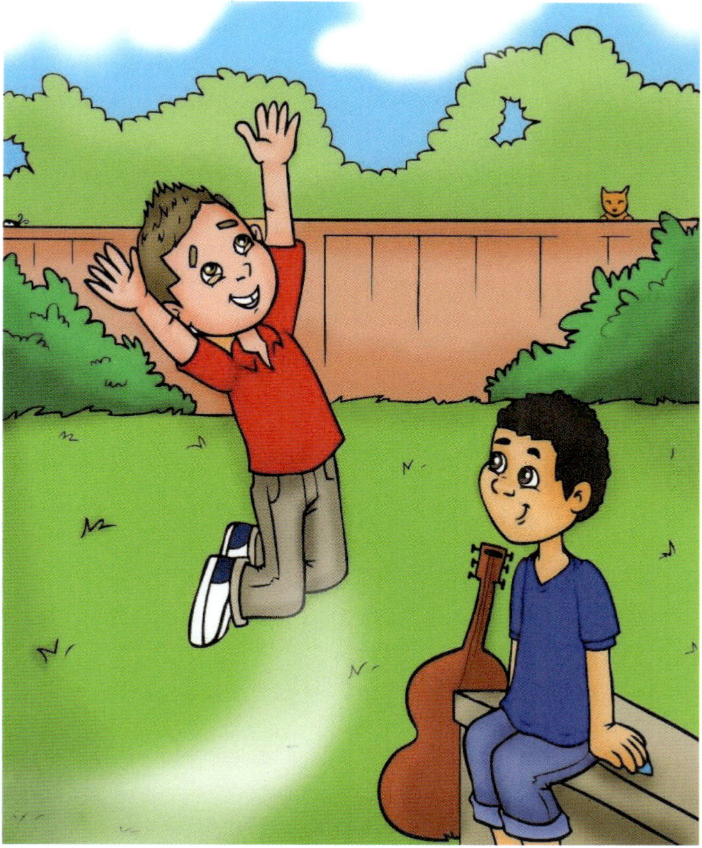

LOVE

MAKE A NEW START BY OPENING YOUR HEART
MAKE A FRIEND TODAY AND SHOW THE WAY
DON'T BE IN DOUBT, LEAVE NO-ONE OUT
IT'S COOL TO BE KIND
ABC, I LOVE ME

LOVE

Seeing you, like I see me
I see we are the same
Not in looks, not in name
But in our hearts, there's a flame.

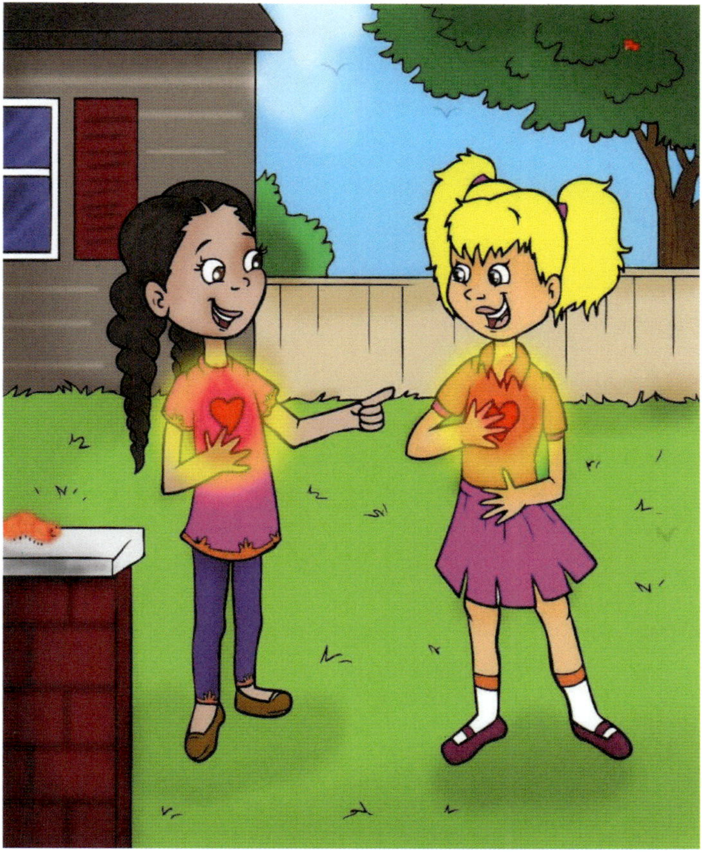

LOVE

The flame in our hearts grows with love
But where do we find it? from up above?
Some places I know of where you can look
You're sure to find it by hook or by crook.

Start with school, make a friend, it's always a start
Then another and another 'til you're all taking part
Make a big friendship ring that goes round the school
No-one's left out and everyone's cool.

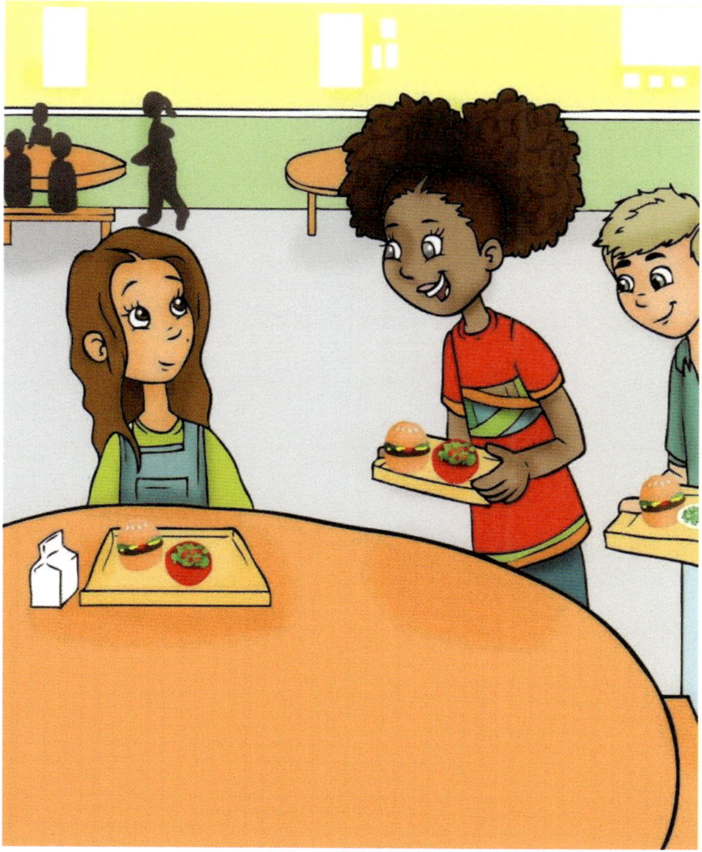

PEACE

HAPPINESS IS A STATE OF MIND
KNOW YOURSELF
BE TRUE TO YOURSELF
SAYING THANK YOU BRINGS PEACE
I KNOW I AM LOVED

PEACE

Peace comes in waves
Just like the sea
When I think happy thoughts
Or enjoy being me.

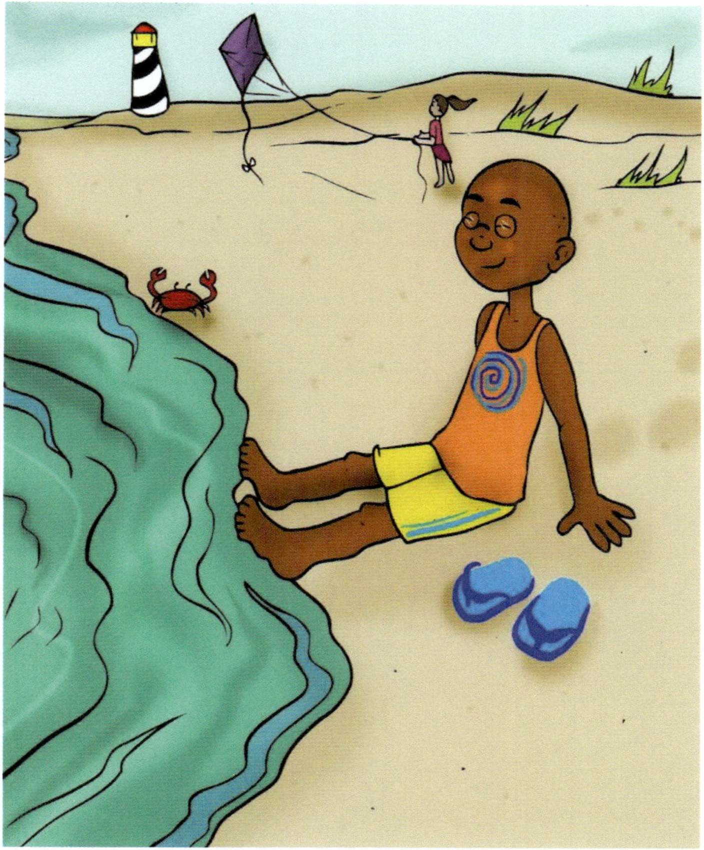

PEACE

Most people like buying new things
They think it makes them feel good
But for some in this world who are hungry and poor
The only thing they want is food.

We waste so much every day
Things we don't really need
It's the poor in this world who really know
Peace is the opposite of greed.

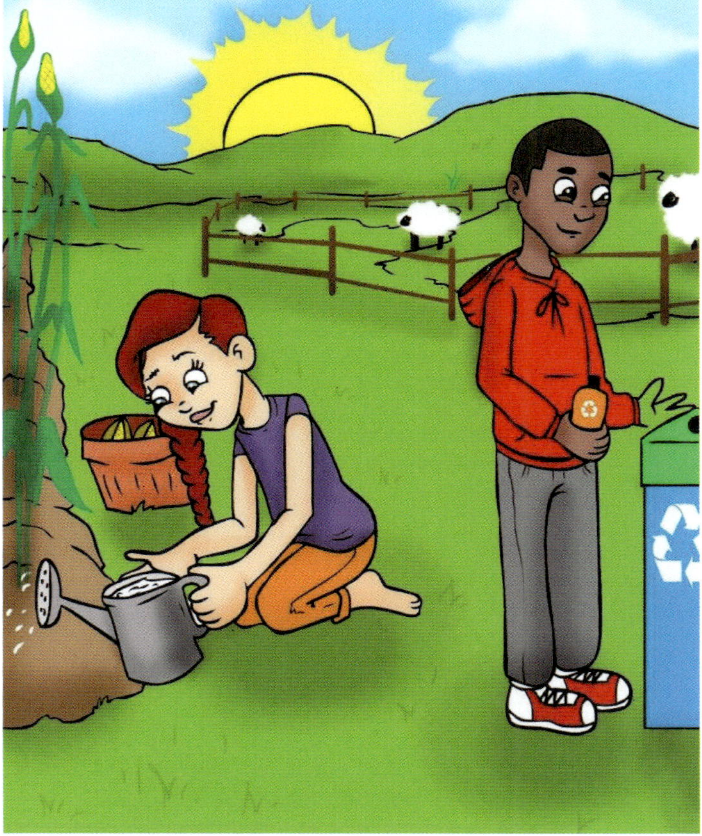

RIGHT-CONDUCT

IT'S NOT COOL TO BE A FOOL
SHARE A SMILE
SHARE A LAUGH
BE KIND TO YOURSELF
WE CAN LEARN FROM MISTAKES

RIGHT-CONDUCT

A promise I make to you from me
I will treat you like me, just the same
And what I do to you, I do to me
And then there's no-one to blame.

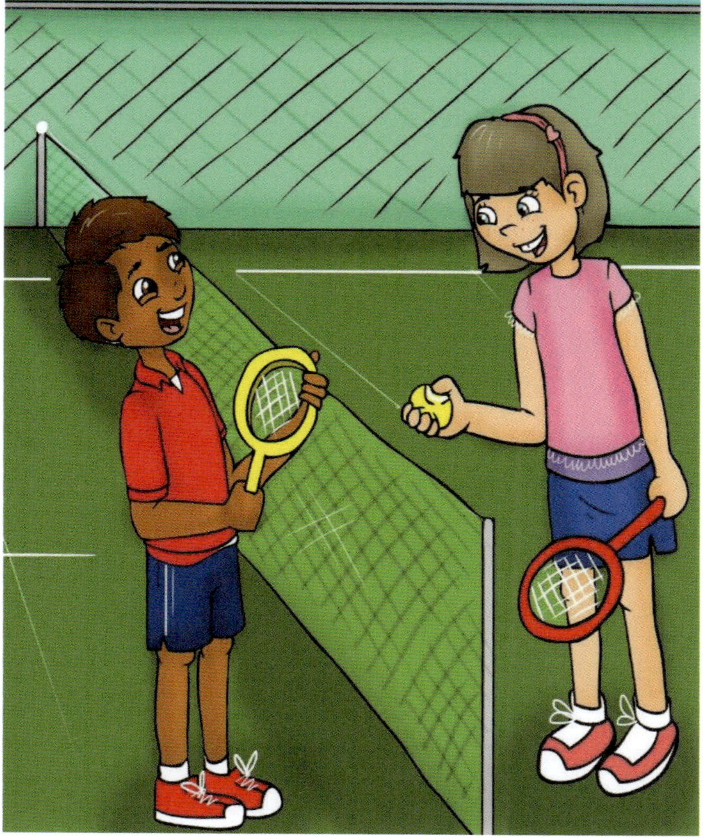

RIGHT-CONDUCT

Whatever we do with our life
It's always important to know
That to do your best and speak the truth
Is what helps us to grow

23

NON-VIOLENCE

THE HUMAN RACE IS ONE BIG FAMILY
CALM THOUGHTS MEAN CALM ACTIONS
I'M GOOD ENOUGH, YOU'RE GOOD ENOUGH
I CONTROL MY OWN THOUGHTS
IT'S BETTER TO BE KIND THAN TO BE RIGHT

NON-VIOLENCE

I know I'm in control of me
I don't need to prove I'm right
I'm calm inside with a smile on my face
This always avoids a fight.

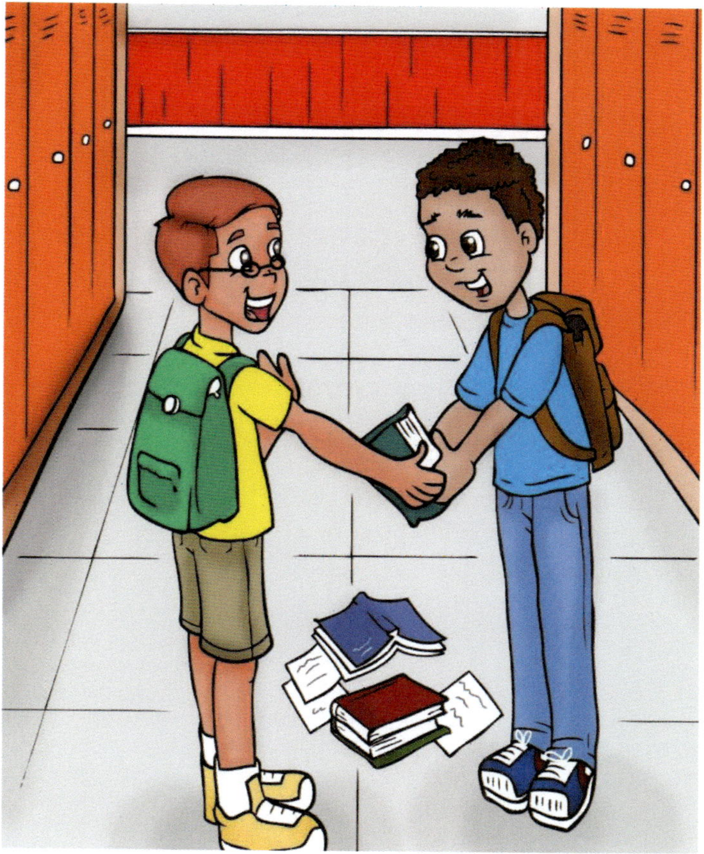

NON-VIOLENCE

We all need to think of the part that we play
In things that happen to us
It's good to remember every day
To learn to forgive and to trust.

See the world as a kind place
It's on your side, even if it doesn't look that way
There are always kind people of every race
Who keep love alive every day.

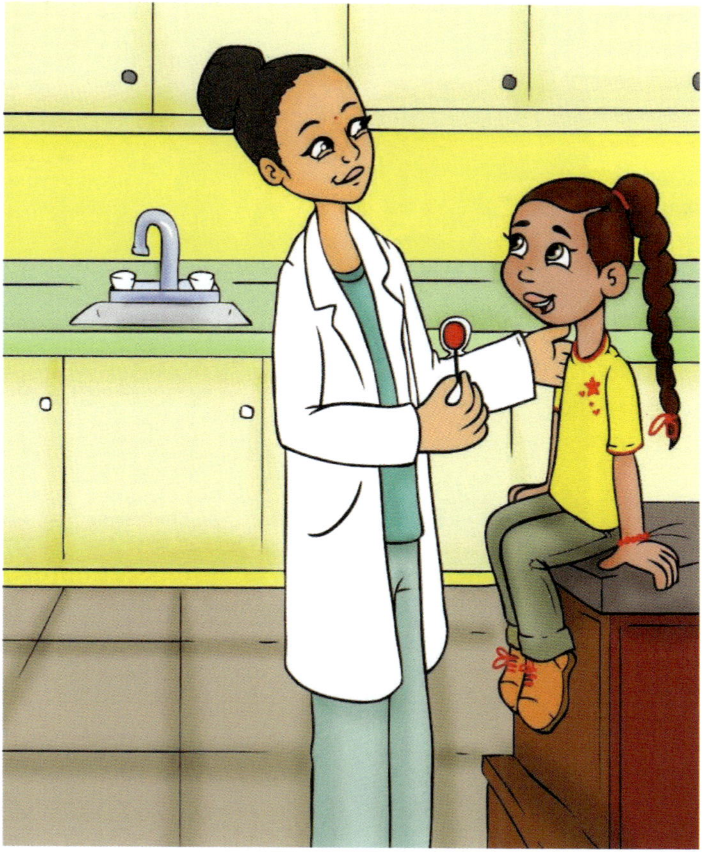

ACKNOWLEDGEMENT

The idea for the five values came from my work with the Human Values Foundation.

Gloria Prema

BSc., Dip.Env.& Dev., MNFSH

September 2020

Printed in Great Britain
by Amazon